# The Bibliography of Izaak Walton's Compleat Angler

By

Thomas Satchell

Published by Forgotten Books 2012

Originally Published 1882

PIBN 1000124667

The Bibliography of

# IZAAK WALTON'S COMPLEAT ANGLER

BY

THOMAS SATCHELL.

*(An excerpt from the "Bibliotheca Piscatoria" of Westwood and Satchell, printed for presentation only.)*

LONDON :

1882.

*35.*

The Hon: J. Russell Lowell
D. C. L.

with M Satchell's respects.

Hampstead: April 20th 1882.

Printed by PEYTON & CO., 11, Bartholomew Close, E.C.

# THE BIBLIOGRAPHY

OF

# THE COMPLEAT ANGLER.

**Walton (Izaak.)** The compleat angler or the contempla-tive man's recreation. Being a discourse of fish and fishing, not unworthy the perusal of most anglers. Simon Peter said, I go a fishing : and they said, we also wil go with thee. John 21. 3. London, printed by T. Maxey for Rich. Marriot, in S. Dunstans Church-yard, Fleet-street, 1653. 8°.

[ Collation : A–R 3 in eights ; or pp. xvi. 246. The first sentence of the title is engraved on scroll, with dolphins above and below, and clusters of fish pendant on either side. Very neat engravings of the trout, pike, carp, tench, perch, and barbel are inserted in the text. The engraver is unknown, but Pierre Lombart, a noted Frenchman then resident in this country and engaged in illustrating books, and also Faithorne and Vaughan are possible candidates for the honour. We know that the last mentioned was employed by Marriot on other work. These plates which are said, with little probability, to have been of silver, served for the first four editions, and were re-engraved in reverse, by a less artistic hand, for the fifth impression, a circumstance which has escaped notice.

"The compleat angler" was published in the beginning of the month of May and the first trace of its existence is found in an advertisement on the last page (2716) of no. 179 of "The Perfect Diurnal... From Munday May 9 to Munday May 16, 1652," [1653]. There are five book advertisements, and one of the loss of two geldings, in this number. The second as follows : "The *compleat angler*, or the *Contemplative man's Recreation*, being a Dis-course of Fish and Fishing, not unworthy the perusal of most Anglers, of 18 pence price. Written by Iz. Wa. Also the known play of the *Spanish Gipsee*, never till now published. Both printed for Richard Marriot, to be sold at his shop in Saint Dunstans Church-yard, Fleet street." Another advertisement, beginning "There is

newly extant, a Book of 18d. price, called the *Compleat angler, etc* "
is found at the foot of the last page (1470) of no. 154 of the " Mer-
curius Politicus... From Thursday, May 19 to Thursday May 26,
1653 "

The " Epistle dedicatory," addressed " To the right worshipful
John Offley of Madeley Manor in the County of Stafford, Esq." is
signed " Iz. Wa.," and the author's name does not appear on the
title-page before the edition of 1676. The commendatory verses in
the second edition are, however, inscribed to " Mr. Izaak Walton."

A fine and perfect copy of the first edition, estimated by Dr.
Bethune in 1847 at twelve guineas, is now worth £50 to £60, an
enhancement of value in which the other editions have not parti-
cipated. This advance will probably continue, for the number of
collectors has increased and is increasing with whom the rule
obtains, "aut Cæsar, aut nullus." A FIRST Walton confers dis-
tinction upon its owner. A Second is but a *Second*, though it may
be rarer. If a copy be perfect, its condition somewhat affects
its value, but an imperfect copy seeks a market in vain save at a low
price. We forbear quoting auction prices. Copies rarely reach the
auction room and the prices, at which they may have been occa-
sionally sold there, afford no criterion of their true value.]

The compleat angler or the contemplative man's
recreation. Being a discourse of rivers, and fish-ponds, and
fish, and fishing. Not unworthy the perusal of most anglers.
The second edition much enlarged. John 21. 3. Simon Peter
saith unto them, I go a fishing, they said unto him, we also go
with thee. London, printed by T. M. for Rich. Marriot, and
are to be sold at his shop in St. Dunstans Church-yard Fleet-
street. 1655. 12°.

[ Collation: A to Q in 12s.; or, pp. xxiv, 355, i (blank), iii (Contents),
i (blank.) The engraved scroll is again used on title and to the plates
of fish are added the bream, the eel, the loach and the bull-head.
The book has almost been rewritten. The interlocutors are three
in this edition, Piscator, Auceps, and Venator who takes the place
of Viator. Commendatory verses by seven writers are for the first
time inserted. The first " To my dear brother-in-law Mr. Izaak
Walton " is signed " Jo. Floud, Mr. of Arts ;" the next " C. H.,
Mr. of Arts," that is " Ch. Harvie " as given in 1676 ; then follow
" Tho. Weaver, Mr. of Arts," " Edw. Powel, Master of Arts,"
" Alex. Brome," " Rob. Floud C.," and " Henry Bayley, Artium
Magister." ]

The compleat angler or the contemplative man's
recreation. Being a discourse of rivers, fish-ponds, fish and
fishing. To which is added the laws of angling : with a new
table of the particulars in this book. The third edition much
enlarged. London, printed by J. G. for Rich. Marriot, at his
shop in St. Dunstans Church-yard, Fleet-street. 1661. 8°.

[ Collation : A to s in eights ; or pp. xvi, 255, i (blank), vii ( The
laws of angling), i (blank), viii (Contents and Table). The engraved
scroll is again used. The changes in the body of the work are few

and unimportant. Brome's commendatory verses are omitted, and the Laws of angling and a Table of contents added. A copy of this edition, once at Chatsworth, formerly belonged to Charles the Second, of "merry" memory, who was an angler as Rochester's verses, quoted at p. 178, intimate in an unworthy sneer. It bears the royal autograph : "car : Rex," on the engraved title. The Walton entries in the sumptuous catalogue of this library are among the curiosities of bibliographical literature. This particular copy is apparently assigned to the year 1667.]

. The complete angler, or the contemplative man's recreation. Being a discourse of rivers, fish-ponds, fish and fishing... The third edition much enlarged. London, printed for R. Marriot, and are to be sold by Simon Gape neer the Inner Temple-Gate in Fleet-street. 1664. 8°.
[ Copies of the 1661 edition with a fresh title-page.]

. The compleat angler or the contemplative man's recreation. Being a discourse of rivers, fish-ponds, fish, and fishing...The fourth edition, much corrected and enlarged. London, printed for R. Marriot, and are to be sold by Charles Harper, at his shop the next door to the Crown near Ser-geants-Inn in Chancery-lane, 1668. 8°.
[ Collation : A to s in eights ; or pp. xvi. 255, i (blank), vii (The laws of angling), i (blank), viii (Contents and Table). A paginary reprint of the preceding edition.]

. The compleat angler or the contemplative man's recreation. The first part. Part I. Being a discourse of rivers, fish-ponds, fish and fishing. Written by Izaak Walton. The fifth edition much corrected and enlarged. London, printed for Richard Marriott, 1676. 8°.
[ The scroll has, on this occasion been "worked over," much to its detriment, and " The first part" engraved beneath it. The works of Cotton and Venables, the former in its first, the latter in its fourth impression, were also appended to Walton, and issued under the following collective title :]
The universal angler, made so, by three books of fishing. The first by Mr. Izaak Walton ; the second by Charles Cotton Esq.; the third by Col. Robert Venables. All which may be bound together, or sold each of them severally. London, printed for Richard Marriott, and sold by most booksellers. 1676. 8°.
[ The second and third parts have the titles given under the names of their respective authors and each part has a separate register and pagination. The collation of Part one is : A to v3 in eights ; or pp. xxiv, 275, vii. (Laws of angling), and ii (Contents). Following the collective is a half-title with a blank space left for the scroll: "Part I. Being a discourse of rivers, fish-ponds, fish and fishing. Written by Izaak Walton. The fifth edition, much corrected and enlarged London, printed for R. Marriot, and are to be sold by Charles Harper

at his shop, the next door to the Crown near Sergeants-Inn in Chancery Lane. 1676."

This is the last edition published during the author's lifetime and has " Laudatorum carmina," signed " Jaco. Dup. D.D.," *i.e.* Dr. James Duport, Professor of Greek in Cambridge University.

The five editions have sold at Haworth's £18 12s. 6d.; at Milner's £30 9s.; at Higgs's £25 2s. 6d.; at Cotton's £56 17s.; and at Prince's £50 12s. More recently they have produced upwards of £100. We may fix their value between this sum and £80, and refer to our note on the present price of the first edition.]

The compleat angler : or, contemplative man's recreation. In two parts. Containing, I. A large and particular account of rivers, fish-ponds, fish, and fishing : written by the ingenious and celebrated Mr. Isaac Walton. II. The best and fullest instructions how to angle for a trout and grayling in a clear stream. By Charles Cotton, Esq.; and published by Mr. Walton. Comprising all that has been accounted valuable, instructive, or curious, that has ever appeared on this subject. Interspersed with a variety of practical experiments ; learned observations ; beautiful descriptions ; philosophical, moral, and religious reflections ; pieces of innocent mirth and humour ; poetical compositions, *etc.*, so as to render it entertaining to readers of every taste and character whatsoever : with exact representations of all the fish, and the addition of several copper plates, designed as an embellishment to the work. Carefully and correctly published, from the best editions, with a number of occasional notes. By Moses Browne, author of Piscatory Eclogues. To which are added, the laws of angling ; and an appendix, shewing at one view, the most proper rivers, particular haunts, baits; their seasons, and hours in the day of biting ; general directions in practice, for every kind of fish that is to be angled for ; alphabetically disposed, in a method peculiarly useful, and never yet attempted. With short rules concerning the tackle, baits, the several ways of fishing, and weather proper for angling. London: printed and sold by Henry Kent, at the printing-office in Finch-Lane, near the Royal Exchange, 1750. 12°.

[ Collation : pp. xvi, 312. viii ( Index) with frontispiece by H. Burgh and five separate illustrations, and cuts of fish in text. Browne's editing was done with gusto ; unfortunately the whim took him to prune and polish his author's style ; to suppress passages in his prose, to smooth down roughnesses in his rhymes, and to adapt him to the over-refined and artificial taste of the day, a sacrilege all reverent lovers of old Isaac will find it hard to condone.]

The compleat angler : or, contemplative man's recreation. In two parts. By the ingenious and celebrated Mr. Isaac Walton and Charles Cotton, Esq.; I. Being a discourse of rivers, fish-ponds, fish, and fishing. II. Instructions how to angle for a trout or grayling in a clear stream. Correctly and very accurately published. (With draughts of all the fish ; ornamented with a number of copper plates, and a great variety of useful and copious notes.) By Moses Browne, author of Piscatory eclogues, *etc.* The seventh edition, very much amended and improved. With the laws that concern angling. And an appendix, which shews at one view, the proper rivers, haunts, baits, seasons, and hours of biting: general directions, *etc.,* for every fish that is to be angled for ; alphabetically digested, in a method singularly useful, and never yet attempted. With short rules relating to the tackle, baits, several ways of angling, and weather improper and proper for the sport. The whole comprising all that is valuable, instructing or curious, that has appeared on the subject. Peter saith unto them,...John xxi. 3. London: printed and sold by Henry Kent, *etc.* 1759. 12°.

[ Collation : frontispiece, pp. xxiv, 216 ; *front.,* pt. 2 ; pp. 217–340, viii ( Index), and 8 plates. The preface has been rewritten, the "directions for the sport" have been distinguished by "particular marks" and four new engravings also by Burgh have been added. The plates used in the former edition have been re-engraved but the artist's name is not attached to them. This is also the case with one of the new plates.]

The complete angler: or, contemplative man's recreation. Being a discourse on rivers, fish-ponds, fish, and fishing. In two parts. The first written by Mr. Izaak Walton, the second by Charles Cotton, Esq.; To which are now prefixed, the lives of the authors. Illustrated with cuts of the several kinds of river-fish, and of the implements used in angling, views of the principal scenes described in the book, and notes historical, critical and explanatory. London : printed only for Thomas Hope, at the Bible and Anchor, opposite the North Gate of the Royal Exchange, Threadneedle-street ; and sold by him and Sackville Parker, at Oxford ; Richard Matthews, at Cambridge ; and Samuel Trimmer, at Derby. 1760. 8°.

[ Collation : frontispiece, pp. lvi, xxii, 304, portrait ( Cotton), pp. xlviii, iv, ii, iv, 128, viii ( Index), 14 plates. Edited by Mr. John (afterwards Sir John) Hawkins by whom is the life of Walton ; that of Cotton is by W. O[ldys]. The engravings, by Ryland from designs by Wale, are dated 1759. This edition came into competition with that issued by Browne in the previous year, and gave rise to "sundry skirmishes and passages of arms between the rival editors." Browne's charges of plagiarism appear unfounded. The annotation is copious and has for the most part been retained in subsequent reprints.]

———— The complete angler, or contemplative man's

recreation. Illustrated with upwards of thirty copper cuts of the several kinds of river fish, and of the implements used in angling, views of the principal scenes described in the book, engraved by Mr. Ryland. To which is now prefixed, the lives of the authors and notes historical, critical and explanatory. The second edition. London : printed for J. Rivington, at the Bible and Crown, in St. Paul's Church-yard ; J. Caslon, in Stationers' Court ; and R. Withy, in Cornhill. 1766. 8°.

[This is the preceding edition with a fresh title-page, but the plates, of which the early impressions were remarkably brilliant, have now lost much of their sharpness. The engraver, by the way, subsequently had the misfortune to be hanged, for forgery.]

—        The compleat angler : or, contemplative man's recreation. In two parts. By the ingenious and celebrated Mr. Isaac Walton, and Charles Cotton, Esq ; I. Being a discourse of rivers, fish-ponds, fish, and fishing. II. Instructions how to angle for a trout or grayling in a clear stream. Correctly and very accurately published. (With draughts, of all the fish ; ornamented with a number of copper plates, and a great variety of useful and copious notes.) By Moses Browne, author of Piscatory Eclogues, *etc.* The eighth edition, with the addition of all the songs set to music. Also the laws that concern angling. And an appendix, which shews at one view... rules concerning...weather improper and proper for the sport. The whole comprising all that is valuable, instructing, or curious, that has appeared on the subject. Peter saith...John xxi. 3. Walton's own motto to 1st edition. London : printed and sold by Richard and Henry Causton (successors to the late Mr. Henry Kent), at the Printing Office, No. 21, Finch lane, near the Royal Exchange. 1772. 8°.

[Collation : frontispiece, pp. xxiv, 238, (the last blank); *front.*, pt. 2, pp. 239–363, viii (Index), 8 leaves. This is Moses Browne's third and last edition. It is said, in the preface, to be "greatly improved...by the addition of twenty pages, and of several useful notes." The music was the work of the editor. The plates are the same as in the 1759 edition.]

—        The complete angler : or, contemplative man's recreation. Being a discourse on rivers, fish-ponds, fish and fishing. In two parts. The first written by Mr. Isaac Walton, the second by Charles Cotton Esq. Illustrated with upwards of thirty copper cuts of the several kinds of river fish, of the implements used in angling, and views of the principal scenes described in the book. To which are prefixed, the lives of the authors and notes historical, critical, and explanatory. By Sir John Hawkins, Knt. The third edition. London, printed for John and Francis Rivington, (No 62) at the Bible and

Crown, in St. Paul's Church-yard ; and T. Caslon, in Stationers Court.   1775.   8°.

[ Collation :  frontispiece, pp. lxxvii, 304 ;  portrait of Cotton ;
pp. xlviii, x, 128, viii (index), and 14 plates.

—— The complete angler, or contemplative man's recreation ; being a discourse on rivers, fish-ponds, fish and fishing:
in two parts ; the first written by Mr. Isaac Walton, the
second by Charles Cotton Esq ; with the lives of the authors,
and notes historical, critical, and explanatory.  By Sir John
Hawkins, Knt.  The fourth edition, with large additions.
London, printed for John, Francis and Charles Rivington,
( No. 62), *etc.*   1784.   8°.

[ Collation :  frontispiece, pp. lxxxii, 268 ;  portrait of Cotton,
pp. xxxiv, 111, x (index), and 14 plates.  For the memoir of Cotton
by Oldys is substituted a new biography by Hawkins.  An account
of fish taken by a gentleman in Wales from 1753 to 1764 is added
to the Appendix, and also an " Ecloga piscatoria, a Metastasio, ut
dicitur." ]

The complete angler; or, contemplative man's recreation: being a discourse on rivers, fish-ponds, fish and fishing...
With the lives of the authors, and notes historical, critical and
explanatory.  By Sir John Hawkins, Knt. · The fifth edition,
with additions.  London, printed for J. F. and C. Rivington,
(no. 62) St. Paul's Church-yard.   1791.   8°.

[ Collation: frontispiece, pp. lxxxii, 268 ;  port. of Cotton; pp. xxxiv
(the last misprinted xxiv), 111, x (index) and 9 plates.  A reprint of
the fourth edition, edited by John Sidney Hawkins, who " being
wholly unacquainted with the subject," has confined himself to
making such small " corrections and additions " as were found in
the margin of his father's copy of the last edition.]

The complete angler, or contemplative man's recreation ; being a discourse on rivers, fish-ponds, fish and fishing
     With the lives of the authors, and notes historical,
critical and explanatory.  By Sir John Hawkins, Knt.  The
fifth edition, with additions.  London, printed for F. and C.
Rivington, G. G. J. & J. Robinson, W. Goldsmith, J. & J.
Taylor, R. Faulder, Scatcherd and Whitaker, and E. Jefferey.
1792.   8°.

[ This is the 1791 edition with a new title-page, the title of the
second part, dated 1791, being retained.  The greater portion of the
impression appears to have been thus treated and copies retaining
the original title-page are very rare and have not been hitherto
noticed.  One is in the collection of Mr. Cooling of Derby.]

The complete angler ; or, the contemplative man's
recreation : being a discourse on rivers, fish-ponds, fish and
fishing...  With the lives of the authors and notes historical,
critical and explanatory.  By Sir John Hawkins, Knt.  The

B

sixth edition, with additions. London : printed for F. & C. Rivington, G. G. & J. Robinson, J. & J. Taylor, R. Faulder, W. Bent, J. Scatcherd, E. Jefferey, and T. N. Longman, 1797. 8°.

[ Collation : frontispiece, pp. viii, lxxvi, 263 ; portrait of Cotton ; pp. xxxii, 111, x (index) and 3 plates of tackle. 50 copies are said to be on finer paper. The Hawkins series, greatly deteriorated in the edition of 1791, closes with this shabby and threadbare volume.]

— The complete angler ; or, contemplative man's recreation ; being a discourse on rivers, fish-ponds, fish, and fishing. In two parts : the first written by Mr. Isaac Walton ; the second by Charles Cotton, Esq. With the lives of the authors: and notes historical, critical, supplementary and explanatory ; by Sir John Hawkins, Knt. London : printed for Samuel Bagster, in the Strand. 1808. 8°. & 4°.

[ Collation : half-title : ( "The complete angler. The seventh edition. With improvements and additions, both of matter and plates," with woodcut of angler above), frontispiece, title, pp. 512 and 14 plates. Wale's drawings have been re-engraved by Audinet, who also executed the seventeen very excellent engravings of fish on copper which are found among the letter-press. New views of "Pike pool" and of Cotton's "Fishing house" "taken by Mr. Samuel," are among the illustrations. The new editor ( Bagster himself, we believe) has revised and made some additions to the notes of Hawkins. The edition was printed in three sizes : demy octavo, royal octavo and quarto, which last were published at five guineas. These are rare, the greater part having perished in the fire at Bagster's warehouse, with the stock of this impression. At Higgs's sale a copy illustrated with above 270 prints and drawings from rare portraits, proof impressions of plates of fish, &c., sold for £63. It was bound by Gosden, and the bands of the book made of wood from the door of Cotton's fishing-house, taken off near the lock, where it is to be supposed, Isaac's hand must have touched it.]

— The compleat angler, by Isaac Walton. London. Printed for S. Bagster, in the Strand. 1810. 8°.

[ Collation : pp. xviii, 246. This is a reprint of Walton's first edition, but scarcely to be called a facsimile. A portrait of Walton, engraved by Scott from the picture by Housman, is prefixed. The fish were engraved on silver, agreeably with the common credence on this subject. The stock of this edition shared the fate of the previous edition and was partly consumed in the fire.]

— The complete angler, or contemplative man's recreation : being a discourse on rivers, fish-ponds, fish, and fishing. In two parts... With the lives of the authors : and notes historical, supplementary and explanatory, by Sir John Hawkins, Knt. and the present editor. London : printed for Samuel Bagster, in the Strand, by R. Watts, at Broxbourne, on the river Lea, Herts. 1815. 8°.

[ Collation : portrait ; facsimile ( of original ) title ; pp. 514, xx (index) and 50 plates. This is Bagster's second edition. The engravings of fish are a fresh series. The "present editor," was Henry Ellis of the British Museum. The edition was in two sizes : small and large octavo.]

The complete angler, or contemplative man's recreation ; being a discourse on rivers, fish-ponds, fish and fishing. In 2 parts... With the lives of the authors and notes historical, critical and explanatory. By Sir John Hawkins, Knt. London : printed for James Smith, 163 Strand, 1822. 8°.

[Collation : frontispiece, pp. lx, 383 ; 15 plates. The plates have been re-engraved. They were issued also separately and were used to illustrate Zouch's "Life of Walton," 1823. Some copies have portrait only and no plates. This edition was produced at the cost of Gosden the sporting book-binder. It retains the biographies and notes of Hawkins, and has no innovation, save a fresh Preface.]

The complete angler of Izaak Walton and Charles Cotton : extensively embellished with engravings on copper and wood, from original paintings and drawings, by first-rate artists. To which are added, an introductory essay ; the Linnæan arrangement of the various river fish delineated in the work ; and illustrative notes. London, John Major, Fleet-street, adjoining Sergeant's Inn. 1823. 8°.

[Collation : frontispiece, pp. lx, 411. There are 14 copper-plates and 77 wood engravings, the plates being again engraved, but in more finished style, by Cook and Pye, from the old drawings by Wale, which had been "greatly heightened in the effect, by the pencil of Mr. Frederick Nash." The woodcuts of fish are skilfully executed. Some copies were on larger paper and these have the plates on India paper, mounted. The editor was Mr. R. Thomson, author of the "Chronicles of London Bridge," 1827, but the "Introductory Essay," a farrago of twaddle, was written by Major himself.]

——— [The complete angler, *etc.* London, Maunder, 1824 ? 8°]

[Our authority for the insertion of this edition is the "London Catalogue, 1815–1832" where the size is stated to be foolscap 8vo. and the price 6s. All our attempts to obtain a copy have proved abortive.]

——— The complete angler of Izaak Walton and Charles Cotton :...and illustrative notes. Second edition. London, John Major. 1824. 8°.

[Collation : pp. lviii, 416 ; with 77 woodcuts and 14 copper-plates, the latter re-engraved by W. R. Smith from Wale and Nash. A copy of verses from the pen of the editor, afterwards suppressed, distinguishes this edition, which was printed in small and large octavo, the engravings in the latter form being proof impressions. These volumes were received with enthusiasm at the time of publication, and have maintained their place in public estimation, although far surpassed by the reprint of 1844.]

——— The complete angler of Izaak Walton and Charles Cotton. *(Half-title:* The complete angler ; or, contemplative man's recreation : being a discourse on rivers, fish-ponds, fish, and fishing. By Izaak Walton and Charles Cotton. With the lives of the authors ; and notes, historical, critical and explanatory. By Sir John Hawkins, Knt.) Chiswick : printed by C. Whittingham, College House. Sold by Thomas Tegg, *etc.* 2 vol. 1824. 16°

[ Collation : I. frontispiece, pp. viii. 269 ; II. frontispiece, pp. iv. 284. Counts eights. A reprint of the edition of 1797.]

— The complete angler ; or, contemplative man's recreation : being a discourse on rivers, fish-ponds, fish and fishing. By I. Walton, and C. Cotton. With the lives of the authors ; and notes, historical, critical and explanatory. By Sir John Hawkins, Knt. London, printed for the proprietors [of the English Classics] by J. F. Dove. 1825. 12°.

[ Collation : portrait, engraved title, pp. 420, 4 plates of fish from ill-engraved blocks now in the Denison collection. These blocks, eighteen in number, are believed to be the work of Thomas Bewick. They came from the collection of Mr. E. B. Jupp, sold at Christie's in February, 1878. A few (50) prints on India paper were taken with this title : "Woodcuts of British Fishes. Engraved by Thomas Bewick. London, Jas. Toovey. 1878." 8vo. The wood engravings mentioned by us at p. 31, are in the possession of Miss Bewick. See BEWICK ( T.)]

— The compleat angler ; or the contemplative man's recreation. Two parts. The first by Izaak Walton, the second by Charles Cotton. London, William Pickering. 1825. 32°.

[ Collation : frontispiece, engraved title, pp. xvi, 314, iv (notes and index). The frontispiece and engraved title, both by Thos. Stothard, were enlarged for the edition of 1836. Brief biographies are prefixed and the notes are confined to one page at the end of the volume.]

——— The complete angler ; or, the contemplative man's recreation. In two parts. The first by Izaak Walton, the second by Charles Cotton. London, William Pickering. 1826. 16°.

[ Collation : half-title, portrait, engraved title dated 1827, pp. xxv, 232 ; portrait, pp. 233–325, iv (index).]

——— The complete angler of Izaak Walton and Charles Cotton. Chiswick : printed by C. and C. Whittingham. Sold by Thomas Tegg, *etc.* 2 vol. 1826. 16°.

[ Collation : vol. I, frontispiece, pp. 291 ; vol. II, frontispiece, pp. iv, 264. A reprint of the 1797 Hawkins, with neat woodcuts on title-pages and in text, designed by W. Harvey and engraved by S. Williams and others.]

— • The complete angler ; or, contemplative man's recreation. By Isaac Walton and Charles Cotton. Embellished with portraits of the authors and engravings of the river-fish described in the work. London, printed for William Cole. [*circa* 1828.] 8°.

[ Collation : pp. xx, 314 and two portraits.]

— The complete angler or contemplative man's recreation : being a discourse on rivers, fish-ponds, fish and fishing. With lives and notes. By Sir John Hawkins, Knight. Edited By James Rennie, A.M., Professor of Zoology, King's College, London. Edinburgh : published for the proprietors by W. and R. Chambers ; London, W. Orr ; Dublin, W. Curry Jun. and Co. 1833. 8°.

[ Collation : portrait, pp. iv, 328, with engraved plate of music, views of Walton's house and of Amwell Hill, and cuts of fish, *etc.*, in text. Mr. Rennie was a naturalist, and his notes, all bearing his initials, chiefly deal with Walton's natural history, which the neglect of previous editors made highly necessary. He has not corrected " the errors of the original " without stumbling, however. When Walton (p. 193) speaks of the King-fisher's nest as a curious structure " not to be made by the art of man," Rennie pertly adds, " Walton here mistakes for a Kingfisher's nest, the round crustaceous shell of the sea urchin " !]

— Walton and Cotton's complete angler ; or, contemplative man's recreation : being a discourse on rivers, fishponds, fish, and fishing. With lives, and notes, by Sir John Hawkins, Knight. Edited by James Rennie, A.M. London: Allan Bell and Co., Simpkin and Marshall ; Edinburgh [ printed ], Fraser and Co.; Dublin, W. Curry, Jun. and Co. 1834. 8°.

[ Collation : pp. iv, 328, i ( list of illustrations). Forms a volume of the " British Library," and is a paginary reprint of the edition of 1833.]

— The complete angler; or, contemplative man's recreation :... With lives and notes, by Sir John Hawkins, Knight. Edited by James Rennie, A.M. A new edition. London, Allan Bell and Co., and Simpkin and Marshall. 1834. 8°.;

[ The same with different title-page.]

— The complete angler, or, contemplative man's recreation:... With lives, and notes, by Sir John Hawkins, Knight. Edited by James Rennie, A.M. A new edition. Edinburgh : published by Fraser and Co.; Smith, Elder and Co., Cornhill, London ; W. Curry, Jun. and Co., Dublin, 1834. 8°

[ Still the same. There are probably copies bearing the name of Simpkin and Marshall alone but we have not examined one.]

— The complete angler of Izaak Walton and Charles Cotton : extensively embellished with engravings on copper and wood, from original paintings and drawings, by first-rate artists. To which are added, an introductory essay; the Linnæan arrangement of the various river fish delineated in the work; and illustrative notes. Third edition. London, J. Major, Great Russell-street, Bloomsbury. Printed by W. Nicol, 51, Pall Mall. 1835. 8°.

[ A paginary reprint of Major's second edition (1824), with the 77 woodcuts and 15 copper-plates, a portrait of Dr. Thomas Wharton being, on this occasion, added. The plates are much the worse for wear.]

—    The complete angler; or, contemplative man's recreation :...With lives and notes, by Sir John Hawkins, Knight. Edited by James Rennie, A.M. London : Thomas Tegg and Son, Cheapside; R. Griffin and Co., Glasgow; Tegg, Wise and Co., Dublin. 1835. 8°.

A paginary reprint of the edition of 1833 with the same illustrations.]

—    The complete angler or the contemplative man's recreation : being a discourse of rivers fish-ponds fish and fishing written by Izaak Walton and instructions how to angle for a trout or grayling in a clear stream by Charles Cotton. With original memoirs and notes by Sir Harris Nicolas, K.C.M.G. 2 vol. London, William Pickering. 1836. 8°.

[ Collation : vol. I, portrait, pp. xvi, ccxii, ii ; portrait ; engraved frontispiece ( by Stothard); pp. 129 ; 130 blank. Vol. II, pp. iv. 131–436, xxxii (index) and plates. Imperial octavo. Originally issued in numbers commencing in 1835 at six guineas, or, with impressions of the plates on India paper, at ten guineas. This superb edition contains the variations of all the first five editions, voluminous notes, with original and elaborate memoirs of Walton and Cotton, presenting many new facts. All the illustrations, with the exception of Cotton's Fishing House which is on wood, are engraved on copper or steel. They were also issued separately, in small folio form, as proofs on India paper.

"The illustrators are Stothard and Inskipp, the former being charged with the scenic plates and the views of the localities, and the latter, principally, with the fish. The engravers are Fox, Cooke, Richardson and other eminent hands... The sentiment inspired by a cursory survey of [these volumes] is, no doubt, one of pleasure and admiration; but the after and more premanent impression results, we are pained to confess, in a sense of comparative failure. The book, sooth to say, is a pompous book, and with much that is overdone in it. We seek for our modest king-cups and pimpernels, and find these buried beneath a heap of learned and heterogeneous lumber. We turn the leaves over with a feeling of disproportion, a perception of incongruity and unfitness. Inskipp's fish, indeed, have all the force and freshness of nature, and rejoice the eye ; but Stothard's plates seem to us weak and silly, insignificant, as regards the size of the work in which they figure, and unworthy, alike, both of it and the artist... He was no angler, besides, and the fact betrays itself, as might be expected, in many minute but conclusive points... Again we have an editor who is no angler, a deficiency that is painfully felt as we peruse these dryly written, matter-of-fact, unsympathetic pages... This fine book, in a word, is over-dressed. It is Maudlin, the milkmaid, tricked out in a gown of brocade, with a mantle of cloth of gold... Nevertheless as this monument *has* been reared, let us accept it for what it is—one of the handsomest publications of modern times, an ornament to the Angler's Library, unique of its kind, and perhaps destined to remain so.'' *Chronicle of the Compleat Angler,* pp. 50–4.]

The complete angler ; or, contemplative man's recreation : being a discourse on rivers, fish-ponds, fish, and fishing. By Izaak Walton and Charles Cotton. With lives and notes, by Sir John Hawkins, Knight. Edited by James Rennie, A.M. London, Allan Bell and Co. 1836. 8°.
[ A paginary reprint of the 1833 edition.]

The complete angler ; or, contemplative man's recreation:... With lives, and notes, by Sir John Hawkins, Knight. Edited by James Rennie, A.M. Edinburgh, [printed]: Fraser and Co.; London, H. Washbourne, 1836. 8°.
[ Another impression of the same.]

The complete angler. By Izaak Walton and Charles Cotton. 2 vol. London, Charles Tilt, 86, Fleet-street ; J. Menzies, Edinburgh ; T. Wardle, Philadelphia. 1837. 24°.
[ Collation : vol. I, frontispiece, pp. xi. 152 ; vol. II, frontispiece, pp. iv, 149. An edition without notes and forming a volume of " Tilt's miniature classical library."]

The complete angler ; or, the contemplative man's recreation : being a discourse of rivers, fish-ponds, fish and fishing. By Izaak Walton and Charles Cotton. With notes, biographical and explanatory, and the lives of the authors. London, L. A. Lewis, 125, Fleet-street, 1839. 8°.
[Collation : pp. xxvi, lxxii, 396. A reprint of Major's edition, the "Introductory essay" being omitted and the biographies of Walton and Cotton by Hawkins replaced. It contains 76 woodcuts and 15 copper plates.]

The complete angler ; or, contemplative man's recreation. By Isaak Walton and Charles Cotton. Embellished with portraits of the authors, and engravings of the river-fish described in the work. London, I. J. Chidley. 1841. 8°.
[ Collation : pp. xx, 314, 2 portraits. This is Cole's edition, with fresh title-page. The portrait of Walton bears the name of " W. Cole," while Cotton's is inscribed with that of " Hodgson and Co."]

The complete angler ; or, contemplative man's recreation : being a discourse of rivers, fish-ponds, fish and fishing. By Izaak Walton and Charles Cotton. With notes,

biographical and explanatory, and the lives of the authors. London, Henry Washbourne, 1842. 8°.
[Collation : frontispiece, pp. iv, xciv, 396. A reprint of Major's edition of 1839 both as regards matter and illustrations.]

— Facsimile of The compleat angler ; or, the contemplative man's recreation. The original frontispiece. 1653. (London, Sherwood and Bowyer, 1844.) 32°.
[Collation : pp. iv. 335. No 17 of " Pocket English classics." A reduced woodcut facsimile of scroll is on the title-page.]

— The complete angler, or the contemplative man's recreation, of Izaak Walton and Charles Cotton. Edited by John Major. Fourth edition. London : D. Bogue, Fleet-street ; H. Wix, New Bridge-street. 1844. 8°.
[Collation : pp. lx, 418 ; 12 steel engravings, nine of which were drawn by John Absolon and engraved by J. T. Willmore, A.R.A.; and 74 woodcuts in text.
This reprint far surpasses Major's previous efforts in 1823 and 1824, although these have still maintained their position in public estimation. " The obnoxious 'Introductory Essay'...still sticks to the work, like a burr ; but with this our censure exhausts itself; in other respects the volume approaches more nearly to our ideal of an edition consistent in all its parts, than any of its predecessors or successors. Wale's designs, repeated *ad nauseam*, are here suppressed, and the new series by Absolon...quaint, unaffected and picturesque, have the signal merit of seeming an emanation from and efflorescence of the book itself, rather than a set of artistic notions grafted on it... The woodcuts of fish give the varying tones and surfaces with great success ; and the vignettes of scenery, by Creswick and others, leave far behind those of former editions." *Chronicle of the Compleat Angler*, pp. 55–6. Dr. Bethune says of this reprint : "Art could scarcely go further, and no more elegant volume could find place in a library."]

— The complete angler ; or, contemplative man's recreation : being a discourse on rivers, fish-ponds, fish, and fishing. With lives, and notes, by Sir John Hawkins...Edited by James Rennie...Manchester, Samuel Johnson and Son. 1844. 8°.;
[A paginary reprint of the Edinburgh edition of 1833 with the same illustrations.]

— The complete angler ; or, contemplative man's recreation:... With lives, and notes, by Sir John Hawkins, Knight. Edited by James Rennie, A.M. Manchester, Samuel Johnson and Son. 1846. 8°.
[A stereotype-reprint of the previous entry.]

— The complete angler ; or, contemplative man's recreation:... With lives, and notes, by Sir John Hawkins, Knight. Edited by James Rennie, A.M. Dublin, W. Curry, Jun., and Co. 1847. 8°.
[Another impression from the same plates.]

The complete angler ; or, contemplative man's recreation:... With lives, and notes, by Sir John Hawkins, Knight. Edited by James Rennie, A.M. Manchester: printed and pubilshed by Thomas Johnson, Livesey Street. 1847. 8°.
[ Still another.]

The complete angler ; or, the contemplative man's recreation, by Isaac Walton. And instructions how to angle for a trout or grayling in a clear stream, by Charles Cotton. With copious notes, for the most part original, a bibliographical preface, giving an account of fishing and fishing books, from the earliest antiquity to the time of Walton, and a notice of Cotton and his writings by the American editor [ *i.e.* George W. Bethune, D.D.] To which is added an appendix including illustrative ballads, music, papers on American fishing, and the most complete catalogue of books on angling, *etc.*, ever printed. Also, a general index to the whole work. New York, Wiley and Putnam. 1847. 8°.
[ Collation : Part I, pp. vi, cxii, 249 ; Part II, pp. 210. "Nowhere else do we find united so complete a body of angling-book statistics and so large an accumulation of collateral data." *Chronicle of the Compleat Angler.* The book is poorly printed and the illustrations are from the wornout plates of Major's edition of 1844. Some copies were in imperial octavo with duplicate impressions of the plates.]

The complete angler ; or, the contemplative man's recreation, by Isaac Walton. And instructions how to angle for a trout or grayling in a clear stream, by Charles Cotton. With copious notes,...Also, a general index to the whole work. New York, Wiley and Putnam, 1848. 8°.
[ A paginary reprint of the preceding entry.]

The complete angler ; or contemplative man's recreation:... With lives, and notes, by Sir John Hawkins, Knight. Edited by James Rennie, A.M. Liverpool, Thomas Johnson, 1848. 8°.
[ A stereotype-reprint of the Manchester issue of 1844, with the same illustrations.]

The complete angler ; or, contemplative man's recreation :...With lives, and notes, by Sir John Hawkins, Knight. Edited by James Rennie A.M. London : John Johnson, 30, High Holborn ; Thomas Johnson, 22, Livesey street, Manchester. 1849. 8°.
[ Another impression of the Manchester plates.]

The complete angler ; or, contemplative man's recreation :...With lives, and notes, by Sir John Hawkins, Knight. Edited by James Rennie, A.M. Manchester : printed and published by Thomas Johnson, Livesey street, [ 1849 ?] 8°.
[ Identical with the preceding save in title-page.]

— ———— The complete angler ; or the contemplative man's recreation : in 2 parts : by Isaac Walton and Charles Cotton. With a new introduction and notes ; and embellished with 85 engravings on copper and wood. London, Henry Kent Causton, 1851.  8°.

[ Collation : pp. lxviii, 418 and 15 plates including frontispiece. " Mr. Causton on the strength of his descent from Richard and Henry Causton, the printers and publishers of Moses Browne's revival (1772) finds it incumbent on him to attempt a quixotic rehabilitation of Browne's editing and even to perpetuate some of his 'expurgations,' and all his notes." *Chronicle of the Compleat Angler.* The plates reproduce Wale's series of drawings borrowed from , Major.]

— ———— The compleat angler; or, contemplative man's recreation:... With lives, and notes, by Sir John Hawkins, Knight. Edited by James Rennie, A.M.  Manchester : printed and published by Thomas Johnson, Livesey Street, 1851.  8°.

[ Another impression of the Manchester issue of 1844.]

— ———— The complete angler ; or, the contemplative man's recreation, by Isaac Walton.  And instructions how to angle for a trout or grayling in a clear stream, by Charles Cotton. With copious notes,...Also, a general index to the whole work. New York, Wiley and Putnam, 1852.  12°.

[ A paginary reprint in duodecimo of Dr. Bethune's edition of 1847, from stereotype plates.]

— ———— The complete angler.  By Izaak Walton and Charles Cotton.  [ Woodcut.]  New edition.  Edited by "Ephemera" of " Bell's Life in London "  [ *i.e.* Edward Fitzgibbon.] London, Ingram, Cooke and Co.  1853.  8°.

[ Collation : frontispiece, pp. xiv, facsimile title-page, pp. 326 and 3 plates.  A pretty and useful edition.  A volume of " The illustrated library. ]

— ———— The complete angler.  By Izaak Walton and Charles Cotton.  [ Woodcut.]  Edited by "Ephemera"...  Second edition.  London, Nathaniel Cooke, 1854.  8°.

Collation : frontispiece, pp. xiv, 309 and 2 leaves with explanations of plates.]

— ———— The complete angler ; or, the contemplative man's recreation, of Isaac Walton and Charles Cotton. . With lives of the authors, and variorum notes, historical and practical. Edited by Edward Jesse Esq.  To which are added papers on fishing-tackle, fishing stations, *etc.*  By Henry G. Bohn. London, H. G. Bohn.  1856.  8°.

[ Collation : *front.*, pp. xxi, 496 and one leaf with list of fishing-tackle makers.  There are 203 woodcuts and 26 engravings, drawn from various sources.  Overcrowded with notes under which the text lies buried.  Some copies are without the steel engravings. The unsold copies were re-issued with a new title-page in 1861.]

—— The complete angler; or, contemplative man's recreation :...With lives, and notes, by Sir John Hawkins, Knight. Edited by James Rennie, A.M. Manchester, Johnson, 1857. 8°.

[ Another impression of the Manchester issue of 1844.]

The complete angler; or, contemplative man's recreation :... With lives, and notes, by Sir John Hawkins, Knight. Edited by James Rennie, A.M. Halifax: Milner and Sowerby. 1857. 8°.

[ A similar reprint and from the same plates, which had been purchased from Mr. Thomas Johnson.]

—— The complete angler. By Isaac Walton and Charles Cotton. 2 vol. London, Groombridge, 1858. 24°.

[ This is a reprint of Tilt's edition of 1837.]

—— The complete angler. By Izaak Walton and Charles Cotton. Edited by Ephemera of " Bell's Life in London." London, Routledge, 1859. 8°.

[ Collation : *front.*, engraved title, pp. 313 and 3 leaves with explanations of plates]

- The complete angler ; or, the contemplative man's recreation, by Isaac Walton. And instructions how to angle for a trout or grayling in a clear stream, by Charles Cotton. With copious notes,... Also, a general index to the whole work. New York, Wiley and Putnam, 1859. 8°.

[ Another impression of the American edition of 1847 without variation save in date.]

- Der vollkommene Angler von Isaac Walton und Charles Cotton, herausgegeben von Ephemera, ubersetzt von I. F. Schumacher. Hamburgh, Solomon and Co. 1859. 8°.

[ Collation : pp. xii. 308 and 10 plates of fish and flies. The only translation of " The complete angler " into a foreign tongue with which we are acquainted.]

—— The complete angler ; or, the contemplative man's recreation : being a discourse of rivers, fish-ponds, fish and fishing written by Izaak Walton and instructions how to angle for a trout or grayling in a clear stream by Charles Cotton. With original memoirs and notes by Sir Harris Nicolas. Second edition. 2 vol. London, Nattali and Bond, 1860. 8°.

[ Collation : vol. I. port., pp. xvi, ccxii, iv ; portrait ; engraved frontispiece ; pp. 129. Vol. II. pp. iv. 131–436, xxxii (index). A reprint of Pickering's edition, with pedigrees of Ken and Chalkhill added.]

- The complete angler ; or, the contemplative man's recreation, of Izaak Walton and Charles Cotton. With lives of the authors and variorum notes, historical and practical.

Edited by Edward Jesse, Esq.   To which are added papers
on fishing-tackle, fishing stations, *etc.*   By Henry G. Bohn.
London : Henry G. Bohn.   1861.   8°.
    [ The edition of 1856 with fresh title-page.]

—      The complete angler.   By Izaak Walton and Charles
Cotton.   London : Bell and Daldy and Sampson Low and Co.
1863.   16°.
    [ Collation : pp. xvi, 304, with portrait of Walton, after Housman,
as a frontispiece ; and of Cotton, after Sir P. Lely, before Part 2.
    A reprint without note or comment.   Finely printed at the Chis-
wick Press.   One of " Bell and Daldy's pocket volumes."]

————  The complete angler.   By Izaak Walton and Charles
Cotton.   London, Bell and Daldy, 1864.   8°.
    [ The same as the preceding on a little larger paper.   A volume
of the " Elzevir series."]

—      The complete angler.   By Izaak Walton and Charles
Cotton.   Boston. Ticknor and Fields.   1866.   8°.
    [ This is another impression of the edition printed at the Chis-
wick Press and published in London by Bell and Daldy in 1863 &
1864.]

—      The complete angler ; or, the contemplative man's
recreation, by Isaac Walton.   And instructions how to angle
for a trout or grayling in a clear stream, by Charles Cotton.
With copious notes...   Also, a general index to the whole
work.   New York, Wiley and Sons, 1866.   8°.
    [ Another impression of the edition of 1847.]

—      The complete angler ; or, the contemplative man's
recreation, of Izaak Walton and Charles Cotton.   Edited by
John Major.   Boston : Little, Brown and Co., [ Cambridge
printed], 1866.   8°.
    [ Collation : pp. xiv, 445.   For this reprint of Major's 1844
edition, the woodcuts have been re-engraved and are held to be
finer than those used in the English edition.   The steel engravings
are from the original plates.   There are twelve of the one and
seventy-four of the other.   Only 100 copies were taken.]

————  The complete angler ; or, the contemplative man's
recreation, of Izaak Walton and Charles Cotton.   Boston :
Little, Brown and Co., [Cambridge, printed].   1867.   8°.
    [ A second and larger impression of the preceding edition.]

————  The compleat angler ; or, the contemplative man's
recreation.   Being a discourse of fish and fishing, not unworthy the perusal of most anglers...   London, Alex. Murray
and Son, 1869.   8°.
    [ Collation : pp. 106.   A reprint of the first edition without notes,
edited by A. Murray.]

——    The compleat angler ; or the contemplative man's

recreation. Being a discourse of fish and fishing, not un-worthy the perusal of most anglers... London, Alex. Murray and Co., 1872. 8°.

[ Collation : pp. 106, ii (notices of Walton). A reprint of the preceding.]

· The complete angler or the contemplative man's recreation being a discourse of rivers fish-ponds fish and fishing written by Izaak Walton and instructions how to angle for a trout or grayling in a clear stream by Charles Cotton. With original memoirs and notes by Sir Harris Nicolas, K.C.M.G., and sixty illustrations from designs by Stothard and Inskipp. London, Chatto and Windus, 1875. 8°.

[ Collation : pp. ccv, half-title, pp. 320. The third reprint, on thinner paper and with well worn illustrations, of Pickering's edition of 1836. The illustrations are all printed on separate leaves.]

· The complete angler, or the contemplative man's recreation of Izaak Walton and Charles Cotton. With lives of the authors and variorum notes, historical and practical. Edited by Edward Jesse, Esq. To which are added papers on fishing-tackle, fishing stations, *etc.* By Henry G. Bohn. London, George Bell and Sons, York-street, Covent Garden. 1876. 8°.

[ A paginary reprint of Bohn's edition of 1856.]

· The compleat angler ; or the contemplative man's recreation. By Izaak Walton. Being a facsimile reprint of the first edition, published in 1653. London : Elliot Stock, 1876. 8° and 4°.

[ Collation : pp. x, viii, 246. A reprint with a short preface. " To save all risk of departure from the exact form," it is stated in the preface, " the sharp vigorous little cuts of fish, and the very tasteful title-page, have been reproduced by a photographic process which is simply infallible." It is to be regretted that the process adopted has made illustrations look rough and ragged, which have always been commended for their neat and delicate execution. We fear, however, that the " process " cannot be held accountable for the fact that in the last line of the title-page, " Church-yard " of the original appears as " Churcheyard " in the photographic fac-simile.]

——— The complete angler. By Izaak Walton, and Charles Cotton. Edited by " Ephemera ... London, [printed] and New York : Routledge. [1878.] 8°.

[ Collation : frontispiece ; pp. 313 and three leaves with explan-ation of plates and register : 2 plates. The publishers have issued other undated reprints of this edition with no alteration save in the illustrations. They are unable to furnish any information respecting them and we have failed to obtain copies.]

⇉——— The complete angler.  By Izaak Walton and Charles Cotton.  A new illustrated edition, with notes by G. Christopher Davies, author of " The swan and her crew," *etc.* London : Frederick Warne and Co.  [1878].  8°.

> [ Collation : frontispiece, pp. xii, 467.  The smaller illustrations from Major's first edition "have been incorporated with the present volume," which is one of the "Chandos Library." An appendix at the end of each chapter contains historical and general notes and a practical essay.]

——— The compleat angler ; or, the contemplative man's recreation.  Being a discourse of fish and fishing, not unworthy the perusal of most anglers... London, Ward, Lock and Co., 1878.  8°.

> [ A paginary reprint of Alex. Murray and Son's edition of 1869.]

——— The complete angler.  By Izaak Walton and Charles Cotton.  London, G. Bell and Sons, 1879.  8°.

> [ A reprint of the edition of 1863.]

———— The compleat angler or contemplative man's recreation...1653.  (The Fishing Gazette, vol. III., nos. 93–140.) London, 1879.  fol.

> [ A verbatim reprint of the first edition made from Alexander Murray's edition of 1869, with the notices of Walton from the edition of 1872.]

— The complete angler, or the contemplative man's recreation, by Izaak Walton, and instructions how to angle for a trout or grayling in a clear stream, by Charles Cotton. With copious notes...by the American editor ( Geo. W. Bethune, D.D.)  New edition, with some additions and corrections from the editor's own copy.  2 vol.  New York, John Wiley and Sons.  1880.  8°.

> [ On this occasion the type has been re-set, and Dr. Bethune's matter for the first time presented in a worthy manner.]

——— The complete angler by Izaak Walton & Charles Cotton.  Edited by "Ephemera"... London & New York, George Routledge and Sons.  1881.  8°.

> [ Collation : pp. 313 with woodcuts in text.  A volume of the Excelsior series."]

— The complete angler ; or, the contemplative man's recreation.  Of Izaak Walton and Charles Cotton.  Edited by John Major.  Philadelphia, Lippincott ; [other copies :] London, Strahan and Co., (Limited), 34, Paternoster-row. [1881.]  8°.

> [ Collation : pp. xv. 445 & 24 plates.  A reprint of Major's 1844 edition from the stereotype plates used for the edition published by Little, Brown and Co., of Boston, U.S.A., in 1866 and 1867.  The woodcuts which were (as we have stated) re-engraved in America

are printed on India paper and "laid down" in the text. The plates are also printed on India paper and are very bright and clear. The "List of embellishments," repeated from the original edition, only enumerates twelve steel engravings, but twelve others by Creswick, Cooper and others, all veterans in service, have been added. 150 copies were printed for America and 100 for England.

This ends our tale of eighty-seven dated, redated and undated editions and reprints, with dissimilar imprints.] *

* of which fifteen, issued prior
to 1864 (the date of the

2937807R00016

Printed in Great Britain
by Amazon.co.uk, Ltd.,
Marston Gate.